Introduction

L ife these days moves too fast. Our days are bombarded with daily meetings, transporting children, preparing meals, returning e-mails, studying for exams, or working long hours. Some of us are neck-deep in tough times: friends who forget us, complaining spouses, prolonged illnesses, an unclear path, or nagging creditors. Some of us ache with the deep soul wounds that only come from losing the person that was the other half of our heart. The result can be a disconnected soul and frenzied, frazzled, fearful, fragmented, and frustrated feelings.

It's called soul-lag. The following reflections offer a remedy designed to provide you with a wonderfully refreshing break from what makes you feel "off" emotionally. Each page will encourage soul catch-up through adopting healthy behaviors and habits while replacing all that hinders your growth and damages your relationships. Soul work will take you inside, through activities, questions, and practices, to become inspired, hopeful, self-confident, playful, and loving as your soul catches up with the rest of yourself. Finally, you'll turn it over to Jesus who nourishes your soul as he whispers, "I'll take care of you."

Find a quiet space, safe from all that is difficult, stressful, and challenging. Allow these pages to provide you with something you may need this very moment: silence, so you can bump into yourself and catch up. It's never easy, and rarely quick, but it's possible. And with Jesus, it can truly lead to joy.

TWENTY-THIRD PUBLICATIONS A Division of Bayard; One Montauk Avenue, Suite 200; New London, CT 06320; (860) 437-3012 or (800) 321-0411; www.23rdpublications.com

ISBN: 978-1-62785-130-5

Expect the best of you

"When you fast, do not look gloomy." MATTHEW 6:16

In the Oscar-winning film *Birdman*, Michael Keaton plays Riggan Thomson, a faded Hollywood actor famous for his portrayal of a superhero. Wanting to be talked about and adored once again, he hopes to breathe new life into his stagnant career.

Birdman is packed with life lessons. A note taped to Riggan's dressing room mirror reads, "A thing is a thing, not what is said of that thing." This resonated with me. Things aren't as they appear.

You are who you are, not who people say you are. As much as we don't want to care about others' opinions of us, human nature dictates otherwise. It's up to us not to empower them. While we've all endured the occasional put-downs hurled at us by family members, friends, or coworkers, it's the self-inflicted criticisms that cause the most damage.

Today as Lent begins, make a commitment to stop trashing yourself. When you catch yourself saying "I'm too fat" or "I never do anything right" or "Nobody could love me," change that self-talk into "I'm valuable" or "I have something to contribute" or "I'm worth knowing."

Offering practical advice, Oscar Wilde once said: "Be yourself; everyone else is already taken." Lent is a good time to expect the best of you.

Soul work: Listen on YouTube to Frank Sinatra's song "I'm Glad There Is You." Write down ten things you like about yourself. Then, throughout Lent, repeat these words: *It takes courage to grow up and become who I really am* (ee cummings paraphrase).

Heart words: *Jesus, when I say I want to "be myself," help me act as if I really do. Amen.*

Put them on speed dial

"Take up your cross and follow me." LUKE 9:23

Tiffany awoke the morning after her mother died. She opened her eyes to a beautiful spring day. The sun was shining. Birds were singing. People were chatting in the street. "Life goes on," she told me.

In the face of disappointment, disaster, or grief, life goes on, whether we go on or not. The cross comes in all sizes and shapes: an overdue bill we can't pay, a terminal diagnosis, a deserting spouse, conflicts at work, rebellious children…things beyond our control.

When the crosses of life start to pile up, don't fly solo. Many of life's burdens can't be tackled alone. Don't be like so many others who are determined to face the trials alone. Admit you need help. Say it aloud: *I need help!*

People say to me, "I've finally gathered up my courage to reach out to you for some help." I hear the same thing over and over again. And I understand. I too struggle when it comes to asking for assistance.

Why do we feel this way? Asking for help makes us feel weak, inadequate, helpless, and inferior. We don't want to be a burden. We feel alone. But once we get past these feelings, we can take the first step, admit our struggle, and ask for help.

After you share your feelings and burdens, you may be surprised by how supportive, empathetic, and understanding your family members or friends actually are.

Soul work: Set up speed dial for people you know you can ask for help, no matter what.

Heart words: *Jesus, we're in this together. I'm not afraid to say "help me." Amen.*

ISAIAH 58:1–9A » MATTHEW 9:14–15

The LOL remedy

"The days will come when the bridegroom is taken away."
MATTHEW 9:15

Ahhh, laughter. A good belly laugh stirs the blood, expands the chest, and clears the cobwebs from the brain. William Frey of Stanford University found that a hundred belly laughs is the aerobic equivalent of ten minutes on a StairMaster. That's why laughing is my favorite exercise, right after breathing and eating.

Go ahead and give it a try. Turn the corners of your mouth up and smile. Now laugh. No matter when or where, laughter is always good for you. Not only is it the best stress reliever to naturally boost your mood, but it's free as well.

Lent is the perfect time to get humorically fit. Make a "Doses of Laughter" kit. Decorate a shoebox with smiley faces and bright colors. Fill it up with amusing stories, the merriest jokes, quips, cartoons, comedy movies, and anything else that you know will make you laugh.

When the clouds roll in or you hit a pothole on life's journey that knocks the joy out of you, reach for your Doses of Laughter kit to add smileage to your life. Laughter just might be the best remedy for re-energizing your joy as it shines a fun light into your life again, helping you feel better and revamping that spring in your step.

Soul work: Make a Doses of Laughter kit for someone you know who is laughter-deficient and humor-impaired. Then invite them to your home for a laughter-noon.

Heart words: *Jesus, I believe laughter makes life the merriest of go-rounds. Amen.*

Tricky business

"Why do you eat and drink with tax collectors and sinners?"
LUKE 5:30

"If you mind your business, then you won't be mindin' mine." This refrain from a Hank Williams song reminds us that busybodies and snoops are everywhere, waiting to slither into your personal life, collect sensitive information, and spill the beans to anyone who will listen. They delight in sticking their noses into your business.

These meddlers come across as everyone's friend, as sociable and sympathetic, while they build a "trusting" relationship with unsuspecting prey. Once you divulge secrets, share problems, and openly complain about something, they rush to tell others. Policing your life, they interrogate your motives and question your every move.

Set limits by distancing yourself and standing your ground. You do not have to bow to them or share any personal information. Simply choose to remain private. If they cross the line and get in your face with annoying, invasive, and personal questions, be direct with them: "Don't you have more important things to do than worry about what I'm doing? I don't see how it's any of your concern..."

Dealing with them is tricky business. One wrong move and they suddenly become your personal ambassador of Doom, with you as their favorite object of gossip.

Soul work: Keep the busybodies at arm's length and avoid becoming one yourself through a Bible-quote meal. Here is a separate passage to reflect on every day of the week: Proverbs 20:19; Luke 6:45; 1 Peter 2:1; 1 Timothy 5:13; 2 Thessalonians 3:11; Romans 1:29; Ephesians 4:29.

Heart words: *Jesus, help me always to ask myself: "Whose business am I minding?" Amen.*

DEUTERONOMY 26:4–10 » ROMANS 10:8–13 » LUKE 4:1–13

Misery is optional

"So that you will not strike your foot against a stone." LUKE 4:11

Life can be messy at times. Loss, illness, accidents, and tragedies muddy the water. Suffering isn't fun. In fact, it can be awful.

Author Tim Hansel reminds us that "pain is inevitable, but misery is optional." The difference between winning and losing is how we react to life's hurts. What we do with our pain can be more important than the pain itself. Whining crowds our hearts with bitterness. Rehearsing the details invites sadness. We can opt out of life for a while, but eventually we'll need to make the conscious choice to move on, taking baby steps toward living again.

Often, it takes a huge effort to get moving. But after we're all cried out and the anger has mellowed, we know it's time to open the door and step out into the world once more.

It's not easy. It takes determination and strength to let go, engage in conversations, accept invitations, or simply pull back the covers from our beds. But we're a part of this world, and each day that we spend hidden away only prevents us from the opportunity to live fully.

Soul work: Life is like a cup of water. When it's full, there's no room for anything else. As life continues to present new opportunities, it will consistently overflow because your cup is always full. You have to pour out those unhappy moments from the cup so there will be room for new things in life.

Heart words: *Jesus, teach me lessons from your desert duel with the devil. And when life gets tough, help me to keep moving forward. Amen.*

LEVITICUS 19:1–2, 11–18 » MATTHEW 25:31–46

An easy recipe to follow

"Lord, when did we see you hungry or thirsty or a stranger or naked or sick or in prison, and didn't take care of you?" MATTHEW 25:44

A woman walked into Starbucks and paid for the order of the woman behind her. What she didn't know was that the recipient of her kindness was taking a snack home for a bedridden husband who was dying from cancer. This extraordinary simple act of kindness profoundly moved the second woman to tears.

How often have we asked, "What can I do?" without offering any real help? Have we hidden behind the excuse that we just don't have the time?

Lent is a time to override what-is-in-it-for-me with the Reciprocity Recipe: Give without keeping score. There is no "quid pro quo." Rather, it's doing without expecting anything in return. It's an easy recipe: just show up.

Show up for someone in need. Begin at home: read a story to your child; help with the dishes without being asked; play a game with the family; watch a movie together and discuss it; or visit with a hospital patient, nursing home resident, or lonely neighbor. Leave a thoughtful comment on someone's blog.

If only we were aware of the hope generated by loving acts of generosity, we might do many more. When we give comfort, ease fears, or help carry someone's burden, joy fills our own hearts.

Soul work: Try "Pennies with a Purpose." Collect pennies from your family and others and put them into 32-ounce jars. When the jars are full, donate them to a local food pantry.

Heart words: *Jesus, you know I am someone who can make a difference in someone else's life. Help me to be kindhearted. Amen.*

ISAIAH 55:10–11 » MATTHEW 6:7–15

The clock is ticking

"Give us this day our daily bread."
MATTHEW 6:11

We all have had moments in life that we wish would last forever. Unfortunately, life doesn't happen that way. Unless we celebrate and enjoy them as they happen, we may miss their impact on our lives, for sooner than we'd like, they are gone. Alan told me, "Since I have cancer, my wife and I have forgotten the meaning of tomorrow. When one of us says, 'Let's...,' the other says, 'Yes!' before the sentence is finished."

Nothing lasts forever in this world. We only have the present, the now. The past is gone. Even though it seems ever so close, the future is always out of our reach. We can dream about it, but it is untouchable until it becomes the present. When we live in the present, we're living where life unfolds. The past was, and the future will be, but the present is all there is right now.

Most of us forget that we have a limited amount of time on earth. But the time to make the phone call is now. It's time to say, "You're important to me. Even though I seem to forget, I don't. My life would be empty without you."

Value every moment as if it were your last. Don't just talk about it. Live it!

Soul work: Have the conversation with those you love now. The clock is ticking. Make the most of it.

Heart words: *Jesus, you call yourself "I Am," not "I Was," or "I'm Gonna Be." I want to live in the precious present always. Amen.*

JONAH 3:1–10 » LUKE 11:29–32

It's time for some easy listening

"She came from the ends of the earth to hear the wisdom of Solomon."

LUKE 11:31

Battling severe depression, my friend's daughter tried to communicate her struggle to her parents. As she repeatedly told them her world was caving in around her, they chose, for whatever reason, not to hear her, even when she told them she'd considered suicide. Fortunately, she failed at her attempt at suicide sometime later. Her parents were dumbstruck. "Why didn't you tell us you were hurting and having problems?" they asked.

Instead of engaging our ears, we engage our mouths. We have our own agenda and opinions. Often, we interrupt others, second-guessing their thoughts, finishing their sentences, and composing our responses while they're talking. In doing so, we're dismissing others' feelings. As Michael Nichols puts it: "Listening means taking in, not taking over."

I love this quote: "Nobody cares how you much you know unless they know how much you care." Talking is sharing; listening is caring. When we listen to others, we validate their need to be acknowledged and understood. All of us want to know we matter. When we listen to others, we let them know we are trying to understand the world through their eyes. Look around. All around you there are people simply waiting to be heard. Take the time to listen.

Practice easy-listening the next time someone says, "Can we talk?" Engage your ears before your mouth.

Soul work: Present three special gifts to your spouse, parent, or child: an open mind, an attentive ear, and an understanding heart.

Heart words: *Jesus, help me curb the urge to give advice when I'm only asked to listen. Amen.*

Esther C:12, 14–16, 23–25 » Matthew 7:7–12

Let it out and let it go

"How much more will your Father who is in heaven give what is good to those who ask him." Matthew 7:11

Joanne sat at her daughter's bedside in hospice. Two years earlier, she'd lost her oldest daughter to the same kind of cancer. As she held back tears, I asked Joanne how she was doing.

"Can I be completely honest with you, Father?"

"Absolutely."

"Am I the problem? Is Jesus listening? Do my prayers matter?" Desperation filled her eyes as she looked to me for an answer.

Pretending we don't feel despair or hopelessness is living a life of denial. When we act as if nothing is wrong, we can fool our friends and family, but we can't fool Jesus. He's waiting for us to pour out our hearts to him.

Genuine prayer expresses drudgery as well as inspiration, fear as well as joy, doubt as well as faith. The relief combination is sob and surrender. Go to Jesus, pour out your feelings, let them explode from the depths of your brokenness. Don't hold back. God gives us tears to drain the abscesses of our deepest pain. And remember, you're in good company. Even Jesus wept when his heart was broken.

All done crying? Now give it to Jesus. He's our most intimate friend. Watch what happens after you feel heard and, most importantly, loved.

Soul work: Seal each of your troubles in their own separate envelopes. Get on your knees, lift up each envelope with both hands, and tell Jesus your troubles. As tears flow, drop your arms and say, "Jesus, take it."

Heart words: *Jesus, thank you for the gift of prayer. Forgive me for neglecting it. Amen.*

EZEKIEL 18:21–28 » MATTHEW 5:20–26

Unfinished business

"If you are angry with a brother or sister, you will be liable to judgment." MATTHEW 5:22

Sara was devastated when her father died suddenly. Just two days earlier, they'd had a heated argument, and Sara regretted the harsh words she'd spoken, as well as words left unsaid.

"What did you argue about?" I asked.

"Something stupid."

Family secrets, unsolved mysteries, family divisions, sudden death—they all have the power to create dissension and regret. In Sara's case, reconciliation was not possible. She was overwhelmed with grief.

When we avoid emotions and feelings that surface and aren't processed in time, they linger in our hearts. Dredging up the past is painful. But the effects of ignoring the grief, sadness, anger, mistrust, fear, anxiety, or terror associated with these events follow us into the present, interfering with our ability to be emotionally present for others and limiting our ability to connect.

Therapy, pastoral counseling, support groups, or simply talking with a close friend can help us resolve unfinished business. When Sara spoke with me, it didn't bring her father back. But she was able to let go of bottled-up tears and express unrecognized anger, releasing a heavy weight from her heart and mind.

The past cannot be undone, but when we resolve our unfinished business, we lighten the load on our hearts and minds and give way to improved relationships and new understandings.

Soul work: If unfinished business is haunting you, talk with a trusted friend, priest, or grief counselor.

Heart words: *Jesus, I don't want to leave things unsaid. Give me the courage to speak up. Amen.*

DEUTERONOMY 26:16–19 » MATTHEW 5:43–48

It's time to H.A.T.E.

"Love your enemies and pray for those who persecute you."

MATTHEW 5:44

It's human nature to retaliate when we're attacked, abandoned, or betrayed. But Jesus offered us a different approach: love these people. It's not easy, logical, or expected; yet Jesus teaches us to meet this challenge head-on. He tells us to "turn hate upside down." If you have difficulty with this, you're not alone. The people in his day didn't know what to do with Jesus' love-your-enemies commandment either. It's radical thinking to love people who hate you.

Too often, we reciprocate by hurling insults back when people mock us. How can we love someone who hates us? Our "real world" solution isn't the answer. Try a different approach—the H.A.T.E. way. It will diffuse rather than escalate the conflict.

Halt. Call for a cease-fire. No retaliation. Don't allow anger to rule.

Avoid. Distance yourself from explosive situations with the potential for danger and trouble. Give yourself a "time-out."

Truce. Look for common ground. Focus on areas of agreement, not disagreement. Try to understand actions and motives.

Evaluate. What happened to drive a wedge in the relationship? Whatever the problem is, turn insult into intercession. Pray for those who ill-treat you, and seek a mutual solution together.

It's a challenge to love your enemies, and nothing challenges them more!

Soul work: Reflect on Jesus' challenge. Ask yourself why the act of loving people rubs you the wrong way. Come up with practical ways to show love to an enemy.

Heart words: *Jesus, give me an extra helping of love for those I find difficult. Amen.*

GENESIS 15:5–12, 17–18 » PHILIPPIANS 3:17—4:1 » LUKE 9:28B–36

Check your vision

"Master, it's good for us to be here."

LUKE 9:33

Last Holiday, starring Queen Latifah, is one of my favorite movies. It's about a woman who had a list of things she wanted to do in her life but never did. Upon discovering she had only three weeks to live, she finally started "living."

Do you have PTO-sight or DIN-sight? PTO-sight is *putting things off* by living in a holding pattern of excuses and procrastination, waiting for clearance to land. DIN-sight is *doing it now* by fully engaging in life and relationships.

Each day, we're given opportunities, but we often miss them because we're too preoccupied. Too often, when we pass them up, they're gone forever.

The real tragedy in life is reaching the end without ever having really lived at all. How sad to see people who—fearing the end is near—try to cram all of the living and loving they can into the short time left. Don't be one of them. Don't let this be the inscription on your tombstone: "Here lies Jane Gonna-Get-To-It. She waited her whole life for the right opportunity to live the life she wanted, but time ran out."

Next time you say, "I'll do this later," switch gears and say, "I'll do it now."

Soul work: Is your life in a holding pattern? It's time to land. Give your spouse a hug. Take your kids to the circus. Have that conversation. Try something new, go exploring, find new passions.

Heart words: *Jesus, open my eyes wider to see that every moment is filled with passing opportunities waiting to be embraced. Amen.*

1 PETER 5:1–4 » MATTHEW 16:13–19

The reward of discomfort

"You are Peter, and upon this rock I will build my church."

MATTHEW 16:18

In *Lead with Humility*, Jeffrey Krames illustrates how Pope Francis has breathed life into an aging institution, energized a global base, and created real hope for the future. Reflecting on the pope's humility, the author offers twelve simple principles we can use for effective leadership. My favorite is: "Shake up the status quo and get out of your comfort zone."

Comfort zones are familiar and predictable. Nothing changes. But at what cost? We're held hostage to boredom and fear, trapped in the "I'm stuck" syndrome, hiding behind our I've-always-done-it-this-way excuses.

Lent is the time to stretch those limits. Start small. Switch up your daily routine. Head to bed early and wake with the sun. Change your pew at church. Try a new restaurant.

When an opportunity, promotion, or challenge presents itself, think tall and go for it! Don't allow naysayers to pace in your head, trapping you in your comfort zone. Hit the mute button and ignore their words: "You can't!" "You're not good enough!" "You'll fail!" Rather, tune into your personal pep squad: "Give it a try!" "You're capable!"

It takes a conscious effort to push ourselves beyond our comfort zones. But when we do, we can enjoy spiritual, emotional, and financial growth.

Soul work: Leaving your comfort zone can be as simple as moving to a larger apartment. Then work your way up to the big, life-changing, stuff. Send out resumes. Say yes to a new relationship.

Heart words: *Jesus, I can only walk on water by stepping out of the boat and trusting you to be there. Amen.*

ISAIAH 1:10, 16–20 » MATTHEW 23:1–12

Enough!

"For they preach but do not practice."

MATTHEW 23:3

I once knew a woman who had just about everything a person could want. She was beautiful, well educated, wealthy, and generous.

But even with all her fine qualities, she was miserable. At times, she was so deeply depressed that she contemplated ending her life. How did she get into that sad state? By listening to the comments of critical people. She lived in fear that if she didn't measure up to their expectations, she wouldn't be loved.

Finally, weary of being held back and of the constant need for approval, she found the courage to stand up for herself. "Enough!" she said. "I'm tired of doing and being what others expect of me. Just to fit in, I'm missing out on the beauty of being me, with my own ideas and desires."

Critical people are all around us. My preferred approach to them comes from Mario Andretti. When asked for his number-one tip for success in race car driving, he said, "Don't look at the wall. Your car goes where your eyes go." Your mind will go where your attention is focused. Negative comments stir up anger and self-doubt. Focus on them and you'll run right into the wall. Instead, focus on moving ahead with your dreams and aspirations. Ignore the boos. They usually come from the cheap seats anyway.

Soul work: Critical people need love too! The next time someone criticizes you, simply respond with a compliment and see what happens.

Heart words: *Jesus, give me the courage to stand up to all the critics and say, "Enough!" Amen.*

JEREMIAH 18:18–20 » MATTHEW 20:17–28

The big bad bully

"You know that the rulers of the Gentiles lord it over them."
MATTHEW 20:25

When I was in eighth grade, one of my classmates had a deformity that caused one of her legs to be shorter than the other. Overweight and shy, she didn't socialize well with other students. Rather than befriending her, most of the kids bullied her. I don't recall ever speaking directly with her, but I'm sure I laughed at the jokes and did nothing to make her feel that she had a friend. To this day, I can remember what we called her, but I cannot remember her name. If I could, I would beg for her forgiveness.

The emotional scars left from the teasing, excluding, and name calling received from bullies can last a lifetime. Bullying respects no age, status, or position. Even adults bully each other by dismissing ideas, ignoring phone calls, spreading rumors, assigning bigger workloads, public ridiculing, and social ostracizing. Even if we don't commit the abuse, we're complicit if we remain silent and allow it to happen.

Refuse to associate with those who continually ridicule and intimidate others to subdue them. Be kind and thoughtful to those who feel powerless and vulnerable. Offer your friendship, encouragement, and support. Others will notice your behavior and jump on the anti-bullying wagon.

Soul work: When someone speaks harshly to you, use a "positive-power trash can": imagine throwing away what they said, and replace it with something nice.

Heart words: *Jesus, I want to speak immaculate words when I speak with others. I want to lift them up, not push them down. Amen.*

JEREMIAH 17:5–10 » LUKE 16:19–31

Lessons from the brick lady

"You received what was good during your lifetime while Lazarus received what was bad." LUKE 16:25

After three years, Harriet asked Gene to marry her. There wasn't much time, though. Gene was dying. But there was love.

Gene's boutonniere was a burst of red pinned to the white tuxedo hanging loosely from his frail frame. He stood to exchange vows with his bride. I was honored to pronounce them husband and wife. Leaning on Harriet, Gene made his way down the aisle, slowly, yet triumphantly. "Sweetheart," he said to Harriet, "this is the happiest day of my life."

Ten days later, after a brief stay at hospice, Gene died. Harriet never left his side. Now, the memories of their great love and joyful wedding keep her going. Brokenhearted? Of course! Bitter? Not at all! Harriet has transformed her sorrow into a ministry of healing for others who are drowning in grief, gloom, and sadness. Known as the "brick lady," she wraps bricks in shiny gold wrapping paper, garnishing them with a bow and berries. She gives this "gift" to people who need a pick-me-up, to let them know they're golden and precious to God and others. This golden doorstop reminds them not to shut out life, because every day is precious.

The one she gave me when my mom died is tagged with a note: "My friend, go ahead and cry. I know all about tears. Love you, Jesus."

Soul work: Surprise someone downhearted with a Harriet brick. Write a note, prepare a meal, send flowers, and listen.

Heart words: *Jesus, keep my eyes and ears open to the hurting. I want to ease the pain of others. Amen.*

GENESIS 37:3–4, 12–13A, 17B–28A » MATTHEW 21:33–43, 45–46

Words too seldom heard

"Finally he sent his son to them, thinking, 'They will respect my son.'"
MATTHEW 21:37

I stood by Scott's side in the emergency room the night they brought in his teenage son. Billy self-injured himself by cutting. During their last fight, his dad said some pretty nasty things, pushing Billy over the edge. It was shocking, frightening, and devastating, causing intense emotional pain and anger.

That night was Scott's wake-up call, as he realized how close he was to losing his relationship with his son. In an attempt at reconciliation, he sat by Billy's bedside, took his hand, and asked for forgiveness. "Billy, I was wrong to hurt you the way I have. I wish I had thought of your feelings and could take back all I said. Please, give me another chance."

There's something about us that makes us hesitant to admit we're wrong, even when it's obvious to us and everyone else that we messed up. Being able to offer a heartfelt apology is a sign of strength. Saying "I'm sorry" and seeking to understand why we've hurt someone with our words as we resolve not to do it again has the healing power to repair fraying relationships.

Soul work: Take a deep breath, close your eyes, and whisper: "Is there any place in my life where I need to admit I'm wrong?" Resolve throughout Lent to mend any relationships broken because you always wanted to be right (even when wrong).

Heart words: *Jesus, I take responsibility for all the times I've been stubborn and refused to admit, "I blew it." Help me grow and change from this experience. Amen.*

MICAH 7:14–15, 18–20 » LUKE 15:1–3, 11–32

A fork in the road

"Then he became angry and refused to go in." LUKE 15:28

"You're stupid!"

"So are you!"

"Not as stupid as you!"

"That's what you think!"

The boys finished their arguing and went their separate ways. A short time later, their grandmother looked outside and saw the boys playing together again. All was forgotten.

Grown-ups don't tend to have the same response. We develop razor-sharp memories of past wrongs and carry them around, ready to conjure them up at a moment's notice to use as ammunition. Every time we think of a past instance that caused us great pain, we stand at a fork in the road and make a conscious choice: carry it or bury it.

Carry it. We let hurts linger and have a hard time letting go. We stumble along, caught in circles of anger and resentment, constantly reliving our painful experiences.

Bury it. The second road leads to a special graveyard where we can bury all our painful memories through forgiveness, finally freeing ourselves from the desire to get even. By breaking the deep yearning to "let 'em see how it feels," we can welcome peace back into our lives.

We must decide which road we'll take in order to release and totally forgive whoever has wronged us. It's the only way to break the endless cycle of resentment and retaliation.

Soul work: If you're carrying around bitterness, write this phrase: "I forgive (person's name)." Repeat these words. Don't stop until you get the message.

Heart words: *Jesus, after I bury my painful past, give me long-term amnesia. Amen.*

Exodus 3:1–8a, 13–15 » 1 Corinthians 10:1–6, 10–12 » Luke 13:1–9
or (Year A) Exodus 17:3–7 » Romans 5:1–2, 5–8 » John 4:5–42

Just a little longer

"Sir, leave it for this year, and I shall cultivate the ground around it."
Luke 13:8

A man brought home a little white box from the pet store. Inside was a talking centipede. The following Sunday, he asked the centipede, "Would you like to go to church with me today?" There was no response. After a few minutes, he repeated the question. "How about going to church with me and receiving blessings?" Again, he was met with silence.

Three minutes passed. He gave it one more try. This time he pressed his face against the centipede's house and shouted, "Hey, in there! Would you like to go to church with me and learn about God?"

This time, a little voice arose from the box. "I heard you the first time! I was putting on my shoes!"

We're all waiting for something. A couple waits for their first child. Recent graduates wait for work. Others wait for trust to deepen, danger to pass, God to answer, or an opportunity to develop.

Most of us don't like to wait, but the patient "waiter" doesn't become jittery, asking God when. Instead, he or she joyfully acknowledges the earth as God's waiting room. We're on his timeline. God knows what we need and when. Be ready.

Soul work: Psalm 37:7 says, "Be still in the presence of the Lord, and wait patiently for him to act." Print this passage and pass it out to those you know who feel God is not listening to them.

Heart words: *Jesus, you never twiddle your thumbs or engage in idleness. I don't have to keep asking because you heard me the first time. Amen.*

2 KINGS 5:1–15B » LUKE 4:24–30

Strikeout or home run?

They got up and drove him out of town.

LUKE 4:29

Jesus was being sized by the folks in his own neighborhood. While some were impressed, others rolled their eyes. It was an isolated moment, and as they whispered biting sarcasm, they missed his message of hope. Jesus was up close, and they failed to see what was right in front of them. Why? Because they put him in a box and wrote him off.

His hometown people were acting on the "assumption principle" by jumping to conclusions about him based on one impression and assuming that this was how and who he was—always.

Are you part of that crowd? Do you practice the assumption principle every time you encounter people around you—those you live with, leaders in the church and community, strangers you meet? We tend to judge others by the way they walk, their appearance, parenting styles, ethnic background, occupation, and nearly everything else, especially during their worst moments.

It's the little, unusual details of our personalities that set us apart. When we "size-up" others, it prevents us from seeing the goodness and uniqueness that lie beneath the surface. Hit the brakes and slow down before you judge. Get to know someone before you decide you have them figured out.

Soul work: Burn these words of Jesus into your memory: do not judge! If you slip and do pass judgment, say to yourself: *Just like me! I do it too.*

Heart words: *Jesus, don't let my first impression of someone be a strikeout, because I might need them to end up with a home run. Amen.*

DANIEL 3:25, 34–43 » MATTHEW 18:21–35

The remedy is in the writing

"How often should I forgive?"

MATTHEW 18:21

When was the last time you thought about "that person"? You know, the one who betrayed you. When we pick at a wound, it never heals. It's our choice to live in the land of denial or to seek payback by getting even. When we choose the latter, it's usually a lose-lose game. However, when we choose the hardest option—forgiveness—we can welcome peace back into our lives.

Real forgiveness requires an acknowledgment of the pain. When pain is undeserved, it hurts all the more. At the same time, hostility, and even hatred, tends to creep in. Drain the pain. Get angry. Scream into a pillow. Cry. Allow yourself to feel sad. Bottling up emotions can make the process of forgiveness much harder. Don't be afraid to feel what you feel.

As the pain drains, don't excuse the person's actions. But try to understand their motivations. As the pain dwindles, dump it so the memories of what happened no longer haunt you.

Forgiveness is a lifestyle change of the heart. It frees us so we no longer feel imprisoned and owned by the person who hurt us. Forgiveness gently soothes us as the burning coals of revenge and resentment slowly, but surely, cool within.

Soul work: List the people who make you angry or resentful. Write each one a letter. Mail the letters or dispose of them. The remedy of forgiveness is in the writing.

Heart words: *Jesus, I was wronged. I want to wipe the slate clean, but I need your help to choose forgiveness. Amen.*

Deuteronomy 4:1, 5–9 » Matthew 5:17–19

Be a seize-the-moment responder

"Whoever keeps these commandments and teaches them will be called great in the kingdom of heaven." Matthew 5:19

As Wendy stood waiting for the traffic light to change, she noticed a teenager standing on the opposite curb, crying. When the light changed, they started crossing the street toward each other. Just as they were about to pass, Wendy's motherly instincts kicked in, but she stifled the urge to reach out and comfort the girl, and she kept walking.

Days later, the girl's tear-filled eyes still haunted Wendy. "Why didn't I ask her if she needed help?" she asked me. "Only a few seconds would have been enough to let her know someone cared. Instead, I acted as if she didn't exist."

Often, our own problems keep us from helping others in pain. Other times, we're afraid we might say the wrong thing and make matters worse. We need to become "seize-the-moment" responders.

A "seize-the-moment" responder is alert—noticing the distant teenager, the preoccupied spouse, or the distracted coworker—and drops everything to spend time with the person in need.

Be available when an adult child stops by needing to talk. Turn off your phone and listen. When a timid soul comes looking for praise, pile it on. When a sad friend needs a hug, give them one. Be there when you're needed. After all, God doesn't take away our crosses. He simply sends other Christians to help us carry them.

Soul work: Express your thanks to the people who stayed with you when you felt overworked, overdrawn, or overlooked. Send a letter or invite them out to lunch.

Heart words: *Jesus, a kindness done is never lost or forgotten by you. Amen.*

JEREMIAH 7:23–28 » LUKE 11:14–23

This is who I am

"Every kingdom divided against itself will be laid waste and house will fall against house." LUKE 11:17

The movie *Frozen* has melted the hearts of millions of people around the world. Our parish chose it as the theme of our vacation Bible school. The lesson that resonated most with the children was *never apologize for being yourself.* Sounds simple, yet it's often dismissed, ignored, or forgotten. This should be a mandatory condition in any relationship.

Anna may not exactly be the prim and proper princess we've encountered in other stories, but we have to admit she's the real deal. Her sense of humor and adventurous spirit are like breaths of fresh air.

We honor who we are when we stop being who others want us to be and we peel away our many disguises, letting others see us as we genuinely are: vulnerable, valuable, hurting, hoping, real, forgetful, and fearful. We mess up sometimes, but underneath it all we're just like everyone else, craving love and acceptance.

Claiming your own identity is an ongoing struggle. But do not sell out to others just to fit in. There is no finer compliment than when someone acknowledges that your unique and special contributions can come only from you!

Keep blessing yourself with the magic words "I'm okay!" Then show your true colors. If others can't accept you, then walk away. Sometimes it's better to just move on.

Soul work: Watch *Frozen* as a family and see how many lessons you discover.

Heart words: *Jesus, I want to be my own person and stand up for myself. Help me resist those who drag me down. Amen.*

HOSEA 14:2–10 » MARK 12:28–34

Are you still there?

"To love your neighbor as yourself..."

MARK 12:33

In *Still Alice,* Julianne Moore portrays a fifty-year-old woman in the early stages of Alzheimer's. What stands out about her character is that, despite the Alzheimer's, she "is still there." Somehow, there's a notion that a personality is obliterated by this disease. But, as the movie shows us, the person is still there and in need of understanding and compassionate support from family and friends.

When a crisis shakes us to the core, even if it is something as awful as Alzheimer's, we're still the same person, albeit radically different because of a life-changing event: being fired or arrested, facing a major illness or injury, breaking off a relationship, grieving a death, or on the brink of bankruptcy. During these times, we depend on our friends to draw closer to us, not drift away from us.

Often people say, "When I was going through tough times, I learned who my real friends were." Friends are the ones who are there for us when others aren't. They remain active and involved and hang in there with us through laughter, tears, good times, hardships, and difficult circumstances.

When you emerge from a difficult period in your life, look around, and see the people who've stayed with you. They're your true friends.

Soul work: Listen to Bill Withers's song "Lean on Me" and share it with friends who remained with you when life was tough.

Heart words: *Jesus, I need to lean on you when I'm not strong. I know you will be my friend and help me carry on. Amen.*

HOSEA 6:1–6 » LUKE 18:9–14

Embracing change

"Two men went to the temple to pray. One was a Pharisee and the other was a tax collector." LUKE 18:10

I wish I could hear the rest of the story about the Pharisee and the tax collector. Both of them must have experienced a tremendous change. Did the tax collector find a new vocation? Did people accept him? Did he make amends? What about the Pharisee? Did he live up to his reputation? Did he become more spiritual?

Even though we don't know the rest of the story, we know this: the one thing most of us want, need, and fear the most is change. The process can be frightening. When it comes to change, are you a Talker or a Doer?

Talkers end up stuck in the same ruts. They talk a good game about change and lay out all the plans, but they never follow through.

Doers acknowledge that their lives are out of control. They "walk the talk," and take action to create a better life. It's challenging, but they do it. Like the tax collector and the Pharisee, Doers inspire us with the reminder that "if I can change, so can you."

God is calling us to live, respond, grow, and change. Decide to be a Doer and watch remarkable new adventures unfold before your eyes.

Soul work: Name your habit: flying off the handle, impatience, brooding, needing to be right, holding your ground...Lent is the time to do something about it. Talk to Jesus and tell him your plans for change. Then do it.

Heart words: *Jesus, remind me that change begins when I stop talking and start doing. I want to. I need to. Amen.*

Joshua 5:9a, 10–12 » 2 Corinthians 5:17–21 » Luke 15:1–3, 11–32
or (Year A) 1 Samuel 16:1b, 6–7, 10–13a » Ephesians 5:8–14 » John 9:1–41

Let them go

"The younger son collected all his belongings and set off to a distant country where he squandered his inheritance."　Luke 15:13

Parents are often wracked with guilt. "Where did I go wrong?" they ask me, recounting stories of unmarried pregnant daughters, gay sons opting to "come out," adult children getting divorced again or on their way to jail for drugs. These parents continually travel down the "if only" path. I understand. But when an adult child's decisions and behavior contrasts sharply with your own worldviews, beliefs, priorities, and opinions, that does not label you as a failure.

As your adult children mature, it's likely they'll make decisions you don't fully approve of, but it's necessary for you to respect their boundaries. Some things in their lives are simply none of your business. The most challenging parts of maintaining a healthy relationship with them is for you to not interfere or try to live vicariously through them.

Children grow physically, emotionally, and spiritually independent. As parents, you need to let go of your need to control, and give them space so they can find their own way. The loving father stepped aside and gave his son permission to spread his wings and enjoy life, however he chose.

Let go of the guilt. As parents, you did the best you could. Stepping aside is not putting aside parenting; it's simply starting a new journey.

Soul work: Choose to be present, not pushy, for your adult children even when they no longer have a daily presence in the family nest.

Heart words: *Jesus, I don't want to push away my adult children by being a busybody; help me respect their space and choices. Amen.*

ISAIAH 65:17–21 » JOHN 4:43–54

File it!

"Unless you people see signs and wonders, you will not believe."
JOHN 4:48

Angela and Jason were having dinner when the doorbell rang. It was a state policeman informing them that a drunk driver in a three-ton truck crossed the center lane and hit their son's car head on. Sammy was killed.

"This can't be," they said. "We were just talking with him a few hours ago, and he was on his way home from college." Sammy was the second child they had to bury, after losing the first to leukemia at age six.

Who can fathom the depth of their loss? They wanted to lash out. "Enough already!" Instead, Angela explained, they chose not to let their lives be poisoned with anger and bitterness but trusted that Jesus would get them through it. "After the shock wore off, we decided we weren't going to torture ourselves with the 'why me's.'"

There are some questions that will never be answered. A good person is hit with a serious illness. A child is born with a birth defect. A spouse walks out. We need to file it under "I don't understand it," and then leave it alone and move on with our lives.

The royal official in today's gospel didn't try to figure it out or ask why. Like Angela and Jason, he trusted Jesus. We need to do the same.

Soul work: Visit someone whose grief is fresh. Let them talk it out or cry it out. A listening presence is treasured more than a lengthy speech.

Heart words: *Jesus, even when life doesn't make sense, I'm sticking with you for the long haul. Amen.*

EZEKIEL 47:1–9, 12 » JOHN 5:1–16

Deliberate compassion

"I have no one to put me into the pool."

JOHN 5:7

Gail is living with a particularly aggressive form of cancer. As a young nurse, she knows about giving. But now she's the patient and she's learning about receiving as well. "It's a lot easier," she said, "to be on the giving side."

How many of our friends struggle to put one foot in front of the other? Maybe it's a conflict at work, a nagging physical burden, a persistent financial worry, a relationship turned sour, or unexplained grief. Often we choose to keep a distance, hoping they don't draw us into their world of pain.

Compassionate people deliberately pay attention; they don't ignore someone's tears, pass by someone who is stranded, or fail to visit a friend who is sick. They focus by taking their eyes off themselves and truly seeing what's going on in the lives around them. They notice fear and anxiety. They observe body language. They pick up signs that the person is crying out for help!

"This is difficult for you," a compassionate supporter will say. "What can I do?" Some days, the hurting person will want to talk. Other days, they'll simply want us to sit quietly with them. Sometimes, they'll want us to hold them and let them cry.

Soul work: We all know someone who has been crushed by life. Go to them. Allow them to let everything out. A shared hurt is easier to get through.

Heart words: *Jesus, I may meet persons today who are bruised by life; use me to bring some comfort, relief, and healing into their lives. Amen.*

Isaiah 49:8–15 » John 5:17–30

It's all about the dash

"Those in the tombs who have done good deeds will celebrate the resurrection of life." John 5:29

Rodney Dangerfield's tombstone reads: "There goes the neighborhood." A hypochondriac's says: "I told you I was sick!" Every tombstone carries the date of birth and the date of death, separated by a dash—which signifies a life lived. What we do with that dash is up to us.

In *Souls on Fire*, Elie Wiesel states it clearly. When we stand before God, he will ask each of us: "What did you do with the life I gave you?" Will we answer God's question with regret or with rejoicing?

Will we regret the moments we took our eyes off our lives, craving other people's accomplishments and acclamations while ignoring all we have? Will we regret every time we wanted to switch places with somebody else? Have we been too busy complaining and comparing?

Or will we rejoice as we bend God's ear, telling him we embraced all the possibilities and blessings he lavished on us, proud of how we spent our dash? Will we admit that, despite our trials and troubles, defeats and disappointments, we found the strength and determination to come back better?

Maybe God's question is rhetorical, since he already knows the answer. But let's give him something to smile about anyway!

Soul work: How do you want people to remember your dash? Write out your life's accomplishments, the impact you've had on others, as well as the times you made it through trials.

Heart words: *Jesus, when I stand before you face to face, I want to hear you say, "Well done!" Amen.*

Exodus 32:7–14 » John 5:31–47

From rut dwelling to risk taking

"He was a burning and shining lamp, and for a while you were content to rejoice in his light." John 5:35

You can't help but smile as you pass this sign along a rural highway: "Choose Your Rut Carefully...You'll be in it for the next 150 miles."

I challenge you to climb out of your rut, pull yourself upright, and do something courageous. Be a risk-taker; be bold; take a chance; do something different; push back a barrier. And when you're at the end of your rope, tie a knot, hang on, and swing.

Whether it's something as simple as returning to church after a lapse or something as particularly daunting as dating after your marriage ends, take a good look at what's left of your life and choose to make it meaningful.

It's scary to be a risk-taker and to try something new, because we can't help but wonder, "What if I fail?" or "What if I get into this and realize I've made a huge mistake?" Relax. It won't be the first mistake you've made, and no matter how bad, it probably won't be the worst. You gain wisdom, experience, and character by taking risks, even if things don't turn out as planned. You'll be a better person for having tried. Life is full of wonder and surprise. Go for it. Seek it. Never settle for a second-rate life.

Soul work: Do something you've been putting off or been hesitant to try. Take a risk. It might be the very thing you need to do.

Heart words: *Jesus, I want to be a risk-taker, not a safe-player. Calm my fear and push me! Amen.*

WISDOM 2:1A, 12–22 » JOHN 7:1–2, 10, 25–30

This too will pass

So they tried to arrest him, but no one laid a hand upon him, because his hour had not yet come. JOHN 7:30

A king asked his jeweler to inscribe a special ring during a time of adversity. It was to read: *This too shall pass!*

Adversity leaves us wondering, "Will I make it?" When you question whether you can get back on your feet again, remember, adversity doesn't last forever. Your ability to come back and survive does. When faced with hard times, it's hard not to panic, reject those we love, act out of desperation, make unwise decisions, or say things we later regret.

Our ability to cope is affected by our personality, our support system, and the severity of the setback. There's no surefire prescription for bouncing back. However, there are three steps we can take:

1. Always find someone to talk with. Don't try to go it alone. Talking with another person offers you a fresh perspective and presents options you haven't fully considered.

2. Believe this isn't a permanent setback. Bad times are temporary and surmountable.

3. Don't exaggerate. Give the setback the right amount of attention so you can focus on necessary changes.

Oprah Winfrey offers this sound advice: "Turn your wounds into wisdom." Use whatever adversity is in your life to give you insight about yourself and your relationships.

Soul work: Craft wristbands with the phrase *This too shall pass.* Make them yellow, the color of hope. Distribute them to family and friends who are having a difficult time.

Heart words: *Jesus, when I experience setbacks, replace my panic with peace. I know you'll make everything okay. Amen.*

JEREMIAH 11:18–20 » JOHN 7:40–53

One is the loneliest number

"The Messiah will be of David's family and come from Bethlehem."

JOHN 7:42

Their marriage was in trouble, so the couple went to see a therapist. After about thirty minutes, the therapist got up and gave the wife a big hug. He said to her husband, "Your wife needs this every day." The husband responded, "Okay, Doctor. But I can only bring her in here every Monday and Thursday."

When we stop and think about what we live for and what matters most, we usually think of a person—a spouse, child, parent, or friend.

To thrive and survive, we need warmhearted contact with other people. We're born with an insatiable need for meaningful connections with others. It begins the first day of our lives and continues until we take our last breath.

Building the relationships we desire—making them more intimate and fun—helps complete us as people. We're at our best when we're connected in working relationships with others, and at our worst when we're disconnected. Without feeling connected, we can't grow into a fully human being.

To conquer loneliness, we must have significant loving people in our lives. We need to work to consciously package our strengths so we can deliver clear, compelling invitations to the people who will complete us.

Soul work: Feeling lonely may be an indication that you need to discover ways to renew relationships. Devise plans for spending time with family and friends. Connect with people you haven't heard from in a while.

Heart words: *Jesus, thank you for continually connecting with, and never forgetting about, me. Amen.*

ISAIAH 43:16–21 » PHILIPPIANS 3:8–14 » JOHN 8:1–11
OR (YEAR A) EZEKIEL 37:12–14 » ROMANS 8:8–11 » JOHN 11:1–45

Turning the dial

"Has no one condemned you?" JOHN 8:10

The woman was caught and there was no way out. What could she do? Deny their accusation? Beg for mercy? But from whom? No one would speak for her. Stones of judgment were held high in the air, ready to be hurled by self-righteous people. And then Jesus stooped down and wrote in the dirt. The name-calling stopped as rocks fell to the ground. Jesus' tender words of forgiveness forever altered the life of the woman caught in adultery.

Is someone threatening you with stones of condemnation? Are their words echoing in your soul? "Loser!" "Failure!" Have your parents' voices followed you into adulthood: "Why can't you make us proud?"

Listen as Jesus, the consistent advocate, implores you to let go of the past. Relinquish shame, guilt, and incompetence. Jesus will have the last word: "I understand you're hurting from being slighted." "You didn't deserve to be abused." "Release the bad stuff before it destroys you." "Go, reconcile before it's too late." "I'm with you, no matter what." "I will never leave you." Comforting words. Challenging words. Compassionate words. The words of Jesus.

It's up to you to decide whom to tune in and whom to tune out.

Soul work: Rather than dwelling on the chronic accusers, focus on your gifts, talents, and strengths. Heed the consistent advocates who encourage you to turn your life around. Read Philippians 4:6–9.

Heart words: *Jesus, thank you for never giving up on me, walking away from me, or leaving me at the mercy of the relentless stone throwers. Amen.*

DANIEL 13:1–9, 15–17, 19–30, 33–62 OR 13:41C–62 » JOHN 8:12–20

Look before you leap

"You judge by appearances. But I don't judge anyone." JOHN 8:15

"There will be a one-hour delay," the flight attendant announced. "You are welcome to exit the aircraft."

All but a blind woman and her dog left the plane. The pilot was an acquaintance. "Kathy," he said, "we're in Sacramento. Would you like to get off the plane and stretch your legs?"

She answered, "No thanks, but maybe Buddy would like to."

Everyone at the gate stopped and stared as the pilot, wearing dark glasses, exited the plane with a guide dog for the blind! People scattered. They not only tried to change planes but tried to change airlines as well.

Things aren't always as they appear to be. Many of us become seasoned athletes participating in the sport of jumping to conclusions before we have the facts. We call, text, or e-mail a friend. When they don't reply immediately, we assume they're upset. A distant boss leads us to conclude we've done something wrong. The problem is, these perceptions are not reality. But that doesn't always stop us from acting on them and making unhealthy and ill-advised decisions.

Check things out and get the facts before leaping to the wrong conclusions. After all, you never know where you might land.

Soul work: Is jumping to conclusions conducive to a healthy lifstyle? If not, perhaps it's time to change your fitness routine.

Heart words: *Jesus, my heart feels healthier since I've stopped jumping to conclusions. Amen.*

NUMBERS 21:4–9 » JOHN 8:21–30

Those uninvited pests

Because he spoke this way, many came to believe in him. JOHN 8:30

Two taxidermists stared at an owl, rattling off a litany of criticisms. Who had mounted it? Its eyes were not natural, its wings were not in proportion to its head, its feathers were not neatly arranged, and its feet were in need of improvement. Toward the end of the critique, the owl turned its head...and winked at them.

Ahhh...those pesky ANTs—Automatic Negative Thoughts. Our minds become nesting grounds for those little bugs, buzzing with all sorts of awful thoughts, sadness, inadequacies, limitations, fears, and angers. They put our focus on what is wrong rather than on what is right.

Of course, we can't always prevent the ANTs from creeping into our heads. So we need to be vigilant and catch them when they do. When a thought like "I'm never going to get any better at this" pops into your mind, drown it out with "I'll give it another try."

Jesus calls us to stop being lazy, thinking everyone owes us something, or feeling sorry for ourselves. He wants us to have hope—a powerful pest control for those annoying automatic negative thoughts. Wipe them out with confidence, determination, and perseverance as you look for possibilities in every situation. Hope knocks the ANTs dead by spraying "I can" and "I will." Declare, "Something good is coming my way," and be hopeful!

Soul work: Wear a rubber band on your wrist and snap it every time unhelpful babble speaks up.

Heart words: *Jesus, the blessings and support you send help me through the tough times. Amen.*

DANIEL 3:14–20, 91–92, 95 » JOHN 8:31–42

A tug-of-war! Win or lose?

"You will know the truth, and the truth will set you free." JOHN 8:32

Laurie and Robert were in a heated exchange.
"You want the truth?"
"Yes!"
"Forget it. You can't handle the truth!"
Take two people with different personalities. Add some annoying habits and idiosyncrasies. Mix in some expectations, and slowly turn up the heat while tossing in a few daily irritations. The result: conflict.

When conflict evolves into a tug-of-war over who's right and who's wrong, it's time for a cease-fire. Some couples see it as a time to exit, because they're already looking for a reason to leave.

For others, it's a time to enter into a deeper relationship—to roll up their sleeves and say, "We need to talk. Something's getting in our way." They make the time, turn off all distractions, sit facing each other, and have eye-to-eye communication. Ground rules of engagement are understood, with accusations, blame, and ridicule prohibited. Instead, they preserve their relationship by repairing and resolving problems.

When one speaks, the other listens. Needs are shared, hurtful behaviors are discussed, and agreeable solutions are sought. Holding no thoughts or feelings back, they speak the truth about their hurt, anger, intimidation, insult, or disappointment. Their communication is strung together with huge amounts of caring—so no conflict will ever shake the bedrock of knowledge that the other person matters. Working from genuine concern will heal and unite two seemingly conflicted views.

Soul work: Memorize Ephesians 4:15. Consider it as your only motivation for caring confrontation.

Heart words: *Jesus, speaking the complete truth is challenging, but the lasting results will be worth it. Amen.*

GENESIS 17:3–9 » JOHN 8:51–59

Tag! You're it!

"Who do you make yourself out to be?"

JOHN 8:53

When is the last time you jumped in a pile of leaves or played a game of hide-and-seek? Have you gathered an armful of lilacs lately? Grown a milk mustache? While I'm not suggesting you avoid grown-up responsibilities, I am recommending that you take off your adult mask and act like a child again. By doing so, you tap into your own personal fountain of youth.

We can't always escape the bad times in life—there's suffering, sorrow, and pain—but we can decide to give ourselves an occasional sabbatical from hurt. On this day, stress and problems are prohibited. Begin the day by tendering your resignation from adulthood and engaging in a few childlike activities.

Be impulsive and adventurous! Embrace simple blessings that often go unnoticed—snowflakes falling or leaves changing color. Look for ways to enjoy life's simple pleasures. The evening's moonlight. A crackling fire. Go to the park and feed the ducks. Treat yourself to a Happy Meal and a shake.

As a child, in the absence of competitiveness and worry, we knew only joy. We believed in the power of smiles, hugs, kindness...and making snow angels.

At the end of your "hurt-break" day, congratulate yourself. Phone a friend and share some special thoughts. Enjoy life's taken-for-granted delights. There sure are plenty of them.

Soul work: Make the first day of every month a hurt-break day. Open only good mail and purposefully do something enjoyable.

Heart words: *Jesus, I want to live simply now and then, putting aside the complexities of life. Amen.*

JEREMIAH 20:10–13 » JOHN 10:31–42

Selective hearing

"What about the one the Father set apart as his very own and sent into the world?" JOHN 10:36

Composer Irving Berlin composed some of our favorite songs: "God Bless America," "Easter Parade," and "White Christmas," to name a few. In an interview for the *San Diego Union*, a reporter asked him: "Mr. Berlin, is there any question you've never been asked that you would like someone to ask you?" "Well, yes, there's one," was his response. "'What do you think of the many songs you've written that didn't become hits?' My reply would be that I still think they're wonderful."

God feels the same way about you. It doesn't matter what anyone else thinks. Whether you're considered successful or written off as a flop, God thinks you're remarkably special, a truly wonderful person.

Keep your ears open so you can hear God's gentle voice whisper, "Become who you are—a one-of-a-kind, unique, specially fashioned, terrific, limited edition of one." Shut out the voices of people who try to sabotage your self-worth, put you down, label, compare, or aim to take away any good feelings you have about yourself. Their words aren't true—never have been and never will be.

Soul work: During the weeks before Pentecost, give yourself a TLC (tender loving care) day. Schedule one each month to refresh your soul. Take a nap. Soak away your cares in a hot tub. Fix a 500+ calories dessert and enjoy it. Read a good book. Go to the movies and overdose on popcorn. Pamper yourself! You're worth it!

Heart words: *Jesus, I want to always see myself as you see me—an extraordinarily precious person. Amen.*

2 Samuel 7:4–5a, 12–14a, 16 » Romans 4:13, 16–18, 22 » Matthew 1:16, 18–21, 24a
or Luke 2:41–51a

Rerouting fear

"Joseph, son of David, do not be afraid to take Mary your wife into your home." Matthew 1:20

With Joseph's heart pounding, his fears stirred up doubts about taking Mary as his wife. As panic and apprehension raced through his mind, an angel appeared to Joseph, reassuring him and removing all worry.

Fear is like a smorgasbord spread out before us. It is based in the inherent and unquenchable desire to feel safe and secure.

To combat fear, you must first discover the root cause. Pinpoint, identify, and name the root cause by talking about your fear and its origins. Once you bring it out in the open, you render it powerless. It swims in the dark sea of denial, but sinks when called out of hiding into the light.

Once you understand the foundation of your fear, it's time to change your internal dialogue. Talk back to fear by flipping the switch from gloom-and-doom chatter to talk of endless possibilities and opportunities. When fear starts running its mouth, bring forth your confidence and shut it up!

Fill your head with affirmations and inspirational thoughts that will lift you above all your fears. Your life is far too short to allow fear to run it.

Soul work: Imagine yourself holding a trash bag. Place all your fears in it, tie it up, and throw it to the curb for trash pickup. Then forget about it.

Heart words: *Jesus, I'm going to face my fears, get to know them, and live my life in spite of them. Amen.*

LUKE 19:28–40 » ISAIAH 50:4–7 » PHILIPPIANS 2:6–11 » LUKE 22:14—23:56

The healing power of tears

"Daughters of Jerusalem, do not weep for me; weep instead for yourselves and for your children." LUKE 23:28

A four-year-old boy had gone next door to visit a recently widowed gentleman. "What did you say to him?" asked his mother. "Nothing, Mommy," he replied. "I just climbed onto his lap, rested my head against his chest, and helped him to cry."

Often, we carry muted sorrows, covering them with a pretense of "everything is fine." We hold back the tears to keep them from surfacing. Living wounds are buried alive.

It's unsettling to lower the drawbridge and invite people in to see the hurt in our hearts.

Broken people often say to me, "I'm sorry. I didn't mean to cry. Please excuse me." I tell them there's no need to hold back the tears; I encourage them to let them flow. Then I hand them a tissue.

Benedict Carey refers to tears as "emotional perspiration." Crying, lamenting, sobbing, and wailing…they make us feel free and cleansed. We get it all out like a good workout sweat. When we're crying, our feelings go unchecked. We're vulnerable and able to connect at a deeper level. Crying sends us down the path toward healing.

Soul work: Listen to Amanda Wilkinson's song "It's Okay to Cry." Then ask yourself, "Am I masking the pain I feel inside?" If the answer is yes, it's time to release it. Find a safe place to shed your tears.

Heart words: *Jesus, thank you for the gift of tears. They're your way of not letting my heart burst. Amen.*

ISAIAH 42:1–7 » JOHN 12:1–11

What a feeling

"You always have the poor with you,
but you do not always have me." JOHN 12:8

Our friends have seen us at our worst and still love us. They've endured our anger, dried our tears, and sat with us in hospital waiting rooms. Our lives could be spent looking out only for ourselves, like Judas, the grabber. Rather than asking, "What's in it for me?" we can be like Mary, the giver, and ask, "What can I do for you?"

Grabbers believe the world revolves around them. They hold their hands out for favors, free services, or loans, without ever repaying the generosity. Their only use for us is when we can add value to them. When we're with them, they constantly seek someone more important.

Monopolizing every conversation, their goal is to please themselves and have it their way. Period.

Givers, on the other hand, are interested in what we're doing. They reach out when they sense something is wrong. They let us know they're thinking of us and are there in case we need anything. They call, hug, share, laugh, or simply hope with us.

It seems like an odd prescription, but some of the best times we can have are when we are freely giving to a person in need—without expecting anything in return. There's no other feeling like it.

Soul work: Be a giver. Pick up paper on the sidewalk. Help someone with their spring cleaning. Visit a hurting friend.

Heart words: *Jesus, throughout your ministry you made the needs of others more important than your own. I want to always follow your example. Amen.*

Isaiah 49:1–6 » John 13:21–33, 36–38

From response to repair

So he dipped the morsel and handed it to Judas,
son of Simon the Iscariot. John 13:26

"I screamed and called Ashley all kinds of names," Patrick confessed after discovering his wife's infidelity with her old boyfriend. "She just sat there for an hour and listened."

Betrayal conjures up powerful and painful emotions. It's one thing to be disappointed in someone we love and trust, but to feel violated —betrayed—is another thing altogether. Jesus knew all about betrayal, from Judas cashing in and checking out, to Peter's flat-out denial.

Infidelity, deception, gossip, humiliation, and disloyalty rock our world, unleashing feelings of resentment, hatred, anger, and bitterness. When betrayed, we feel stabbed in the back and walked over.

Betrayal victims go through an emotional process:

Response: This is a bad dream. I'm going to wake up and everything will be fine.

Retreat: People turn on you and let you down.

Regret: I was warned. I should have listened.

Rage: I'm so angry, I could…

Revenge: One day they'll pay for what they did to me. I'll get them.

Repair: I want to be free from this pain and not let it change me into someone I don't like.

Choosing to continue in a relationship after the painful trauma of betrayal requires more than a simple apology or promise that it won't happen again. It takes a soft heart along with plenty of talk and time.

Soul work: When betrayed and working on recovery, wake up each morning and say: "It wasn't my fault. I choose to trust again."

Heart words: *Jesus, repair me slowly and gently, but heal me. Amen.*

The elephant in the room

*Then Judas, his betrayer, said in reply, "Surely it is not I, Rabbi?"
He answered, "You have said so."* Matthew 26:25

A man stopped in front of the elephants, confused that the huge animals were being held by only a small rope tied to their front legs. No chains, no cages. They surely could break away from their bonds, but inexplicably, they didn't.

He asked the trainer why.

"Well," the trainer said, "when they're very young and much smaller, we use the same size rope to tie them. At that age, it's enough to hold them. As they grow, they're conditioned to believe they cannot break away, so they never try."

Like the elephants, we're bound by a small rope of outdated behaviors, thoughts, beliefs, or reactions. As a result, we keep doing what we've always done and end up with the same results.

Two words hold us hostage: "What if?" What if I fail, get fired, mocked, or rejected? So what? Try. It may be scary, but with each step you'll build confidence. Cut loose and see what happens. We tend to stop short of trying something different. Instead of taking a chance, we are passively bound by self-imposed ropes.

Whenever you want, you can decide to cut the rope and reach toward your highest potential. You're bound only by your attitude. It's up to you to move forward and leave the past behind.

Soul work: What ropes do you need to cut? Make a list of everything that holds you back, and cut loose.

Heart words: *Jesus, through the power of your love, I'm breaking loose. There's so much I don't want to miss in my life. Amen.*

EXODUS 12:1–8, 11–14 » 1 CORINTHIANS 11:23–26 » JOHN 13:1–15

Get off the sidelines

"I have set an example that you should do as I have done for you."
JOHN 13:15

"Troublesome times are here," Larry's mother sang each time he was inconsolable as an infant. I think she was onto something. We all face troublesome times.

From out of nowhere, our perfect lives start to shatter, crumbling before our eyes. Serious troubles: an inoperable tumor, a pink slip, an empty savings account, a marriage in turmoil, a child under arrest, or elderly parents suddenly in need of daily care.

It's difficult not to feel discouraged and overwhelmed when these troubles come knocking at our doors. We all face moments when our hearts take a nosedive and our world suddenly looks bleak.

That's why people are starving for encouraging words—"thank you," "well done," "you'll make it," or "I believe in you." It's time to get in the game with others and be the teammate who gets behind those who have the wind knocked out of them. Be an encourager. We all need someone to lift us up, give us the strength to move forward, and help us through our day.

It's easy to stand on the sidelines removed from those who are lost or lonely, upset or afraid, hospitalized or homebound. An encourager draws closer and provides the courage for others to hang on a little longer.

Soul work: Pick up the phone. Drop in for a visit. Text some encouraging words to someone struggling to feel cared for.

Heart words: *Jesus, I want to be an encourager of others and a shoulder to lean on and I want to inspire others to do the same. Amen.*

Isaiah 52:13—53:12 » Hebrews 4:14–16; 5:7–9 » John 18:1—19:42

Tomorrow may never come

"It is finished." John 19:30

Susan and Bryan kissed goodnight and fell asleep. The next morning, she reached over to kiss him, and he was ice cold. Bryan died in his sleep. The evening meal, conversation, and goodnight kiss were their last together. She said, "Nothing helps you to understand the importance of life and people more than death."

Death is certainly no stranger to me. I've lost my parents, grandparents, other relatives, and friends. Death reminds us to celebrate the people we love while they're here—to tell them how we feel about them and to regard them as the never-to-be-repeated miracles they truly are. Make time to spend with your loved ones. Stop making excuses. Don't wait until you get around to it. Show up now, because tomorrows eventually run out.

It's easy to miss what matters in life. Death has taught me that a meaningful life isn't about excellent grades, an impressive bank account, a big home, or the latest fashion trends. In the end, life's about the wholesome relationships we have with the people who've journeyed with us in good times as well as in trying times.

Life is precious. Don't wait for someone to die to change the way you live and love. Each day is gift-wrapped by God; don't miss your chance to unwrap it.

Soul work: Avoid putting things off, making excuses, or wasting time. Be deliberate about spending time with people you love. Listen, hug, and say, "I love you," while there's still time.

Heart words: *Jesus, I want to live life to the fullest, with every single breath. Amen.*

GENESIS 1:1—2:2 OR 1:1, 26-31A » GENESIS 22:1-18 OR 22:1-2, 9A, 10-13, 15-18
EXODUS 14:15—15:1 » ISAIAH 54:5—14 » ISAIAH 55:1-11 » BARUCH 3:9—15, 32—4:4
EZEKIEL 36:16—17A, 18—28 » ROMANS 6:3—11 » LUKE 24:1—12

Sunday's comin'

"The Son of Man must be handed over to sinners and be crucified, and rise on the third day." LUKE 24:7

A troubled youth, Louis Zamperini channeled his mischief into the energy he needed to become an Olympic runner. Serving in World War II, he survived on a raft for forty-seven days after his bomber was downed, only to be captured and sent off to a series of prisoner-of-war camps. His trials are portrayed in the movie *Unbroken.*

Before heading off to the Olympics, his brother, Pete, said, "A moment of pain is worth a lifetime of glory."

On Friday, things looked bad for Jesus as he hung on the cross. But Sunday morning came and changed everything. Jesus, the risen Savior, walked out of the tomb!

We all want to bask in the newness of Easter life. But first, listen to Pete's straightforward wisdom to Louis. We can only savor glory after we've endured some heartaches.

Maybe you're facing serious pain or a disappointing medical report or an unraveling relationship or piles of bills. Most of us "do time" with our troubles, forgetting that in time they will be over. We need to tap into our inner strength and tackle our problems one by one.

As we adapt, we'll have to power to focus on opportunities, not liabilities. Look painful moments squarely in the eyes and say, "I'm bigger than you. I've got Jesus on my side!" Happy Easter!

Soul work: Reach out to a freshly wounded friend, who's struggling to restore normalcy. Offer a hug, a shoulder, or an ear.

Heart words: *Jesus, I'll keep the faith and you'll supply the power for me to keep moving toward Sunday. Amen.*

Also by

FATHER JOE SICA

Forgiveness

One Step at a Time

After twenty-five years of priestly ministry, and after counseling hundreds of people, Father Joe has concluded that over ninety percent of troubled relationships result from the unwillingness or inability to forgive. Here he offers ten invaluable steps to help you take forgiveness seriously, and he has choreographed them beautifully to connect with Jesus' teaching about forgiveness.

152 PAGES | $12.95 | ORDER 957620

Embracing Change

10 Ways to Grow Spiritually and Emotionally

Here's a bestselling resource for all those who want to make positive changes in their lives. This is not just another self-help fix, but rather a self-care solution, a guide to revealing the person we really want to be. It's inspiring, challenging, and motivating!

136 PAGES | $12.95 | ORDER 952486

➔ TO ORDER CALL
1-800-321-0411
WWW.23RDPUBLICATIONS.COM

TWENTY
THIRD
PUBLICATIONS

Liturgical calendar for
LENT 2016

FEBRUARY

10	WED	**ASH WEDNESDAY**
11	THU	Thursday after Ash Wednesday
		» *Our Lady of Lourdes*
12	FRI	Friday after Ash Wednesday
13	SAT	Saturday after Ash Wednesday
14	SUN	**FIRST SUNDAY OF LENT**
15	MON	Lenten Weekday
16	TUE	Lenten Weekday
17	WED	Lenten Weekday
		» *The Seven Holy Founders of the Servite Order*
18	THU	Lenten Weekday
19	FRI	Lenten Weekday
20	SAT	Lenten Weekday
21	SUN	**SECOND SUNDAY OF LENT**
22	MON	**THE CHAIR OF ST. PETER THE APOSTLE**
23	TUE	Lenten Weekday
		» *St. Polycarp, bishop & martyr*
24	WED	Lenten Weekday
25	THU	Lenten Weekday
26	FRI	Lenten Weekday
27	SAT	Lenten Weekday
28	SUN	**THIRD SUNDAY OF LENT**
29	MON	Lenten Weekday

MARCH

1	TUE	Lenten Weekday
2	WED	Lenten Weekday
3	THU	Lenten Weekday
		» *St. Katharine Drexel, virgin*
4	FRI	Lenten Weekday
		» *St. Casimir*
5	SAT	Lenten Weekday

6	SUN	**FOURTH SUNDAY OF LENT**
7	MON	Lenten Weekday
		» *St. Perpetua and St. Felicity, martyrs*
8	TUE	Lenten Weekday
		» *St. John of God, religious*
9	WED	Lenten Weekday
		» *St. Frances of Rome, religious*
10	THU	Lenten Weekday
11	FRI	Lenten Weekday
12	SAT	Lenten Weekday
13	SUN	**FIFTH SUNDAY OF LENT**
14	MON	Lenten Weekday
15	TUE	Lenten Weekday
16	WED	Lenten Weekday
17	THU	Lenten Weekday
		» *St. Patrick, bishop*
18	FRI	Lenten Weekday
		» *St. Cyril of Jerusalem, bishop & doctor of the Church*
19	SAT	**ST. JOSEPH**
20	SUN	**PALM SUNDAY OF THE PASSION OF THE LORD**
21	MON	Monday of Holy Week
22	TUE	Tuesday of Holy Week
23	WED	Wednesday of Holy Week
24	THU	**HOLY THURSDAY: MASS OF THE LORD'S SUPPER**
25	FRI	**GOOD FRIDAY OF THE PASSION OF THE LORD**
26	SAT	**HOLY SATURDAY: THE EASTER VIGIL**
27	SUN	**EASTER SUNDAY OF THE RESURRECTION OF THE LORD**

TWENTY THIRD 23rd
PUBLICATIONS
23rdpublications.com

ISBN 978-1-62785-130-5

9 781627 851305